SPACE DISCOVERY GUIDES

BLACK HOLES

A SPACE DISCOVERY GUIDE

James Roland

Lerner Publications ◆ Minneapolis

Consultant: Liliya L. R. Williams, professor, Minnesota
Institute for Astrophysics

Lerner Publications Company
A division of Lerner Publishing Group, Inc.
241 First Avenue North
Minneapolis, MN 55401 USA

For reading levels and more information, look up this title
at www.lernerbooks.com.

Main body text set in Avenir LT Std 65 Medium 11.5/17.5.
Typeface provided by Adobe Systems.

Library of Congress Cataloging-in-Publication Data

Names: Roland, James, author.
Title: Black holes : a space discovery guide / James Roland.
Description: Minneapolis : Lerner Publications, [2016] |
    Series: Space discovery guides | Audience: Ages 9–12.
    | Audience: Grades 4 to 6. | Includes bibliographical
    references and index.
Identifiers: LCCN 2016016352 (print) | LCCN 2016018566
    (ebook) | ISBN 9781512425864 (lb : alk. paper) |
    ISBN 9781512427943 (eb pdf)
Subjects: LCSH: Black holes (Astronomy)—Juvenile
    literature.
Classification: LCC QB843.B55 R65 2016 (print) | LCC
    QB843.B55 (ebook) | DDC 523.8/875—dc23

LC record available at https://lccn.loc.gov/2016016352

Manufactured in the United States of America
1-41354-23298-6/8/2016

TABLE OF CONTENTS

INTRODUCTION
A BUMP IN
THE NIGHT

An observatory in
Livingston, Louisiana

In the early morning hours of September 14, 2015, astronomers in two quiet observatories—one in Louisiana and the other in Washington State—heard a little chirping sound. To anyone other than the astronomers who had been waiting for years to hear those noises, the chirps might have sounded like some random computer static. But to the scientists at the Laser Interferometer Gravitational-Wave Observatory (LIGO) sites, those sounds were potentially groundbreaking.

LIGO scientists use equipment such as this laser-beam splitter to search for signs of black holes.

The scientists working at the LIGO sites didn't get excited right away. Instead, they got to work. They analyzed the data. They made sure the noises weren't a mistake or a fake signal. They checked and rechecked their equipment. And they kept the chirp a secret. Finally, in February 2016, they made their announcement.

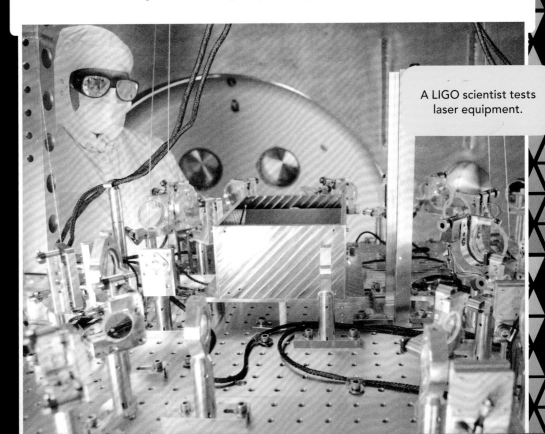

A LIGO scientist tests laser equipment.

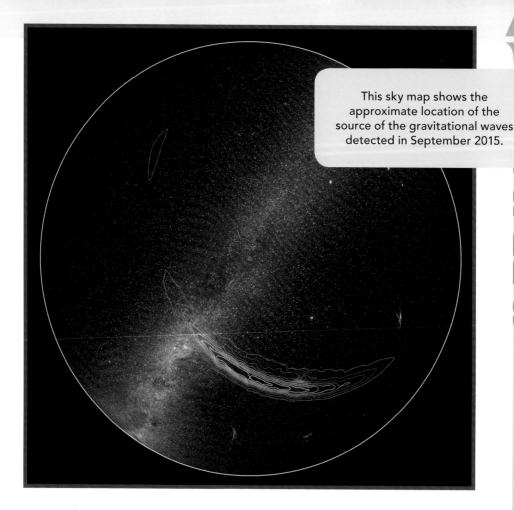

This sky map shows the approximate location of the source of the gravitational waves detected in September 2015.

The chirping noises picked up by LIGO were gravitational waves, or ripples in space-time. The waves came from two distant black holes that collided more than one billion years ago. The collision sent ripples through space and time. These waves finally rippled through Earth in 2015 and were detected by LIGO.

This was the first-ever detection of gravitational waves, and it helped confirm a theory about the universe that physicist Albert Einstein had come up with in 1915. The detection also proved the idea that two black holes could orbit each other and eventually merge. This knowledge will help scientists study and understand black holes, where they come from, and how powerful they are.

The detection of gravitational waves helped confirm one of Einstein's theories about gravity.

According to some scientists, this discovery was the beginning of a whole new way of looking at the universe—almost like gaining a new sense. "Up until now, we've been deaf to gravitational waves," said LIGO executive director David Reitze. "What's going to come now is we're going to hear more things . . . things that we never expected."

Black holes have been a hard-to-solve mystery for years. They are difficult to study and difficult to understand. The LIGO discovery has given astronomers one more way to study black holes.

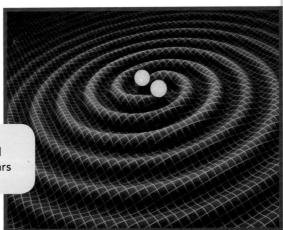

An artist's depiction of gravitational waves created by orbiting neutron stars

This illustration shows what a black hole may look like.

By studying gravitational waves, scientists can work to gather a more complete picture of black holes and their surroundings. These studies will help scientists further understand the fundamental laws of the universe.

"It's like Galileo pointing the telescope for the first time at the sky," said LIGO team member Vassiliki Kalogera. "You're opening your eyes—[or] in this case, our ears—to a new set of signals from the universe that our previous technologies did not allow us to receive, study, and learn from."

In simple terms, a black hole is a place in space where a lot of matter has been pushed into a small space. The resulting object has such a strong gravitational pull that not even light can escape it.

Gas and dust surrounding the unseen center of a black hole are depicted in this artist's image.

A black hole feeds on a nearby star (*left*) in this artist's impression.

But black holes are far from simple. We are only just beginning to understand how black holes are created, where they can be found, and how much force they hold. Many unknowns remain about these dark, dense areas in space, and scientists and astronomers make new discoveries and come up with new theories about them every day. By continuing to explore and study black holes, scientists can learn more not only about the nature of black holes but also about the nature of the entire universe.

CHAPTER 1
DISCOVERING BLACK HOLES

Einstein's general theory of relativity is represented by this image of the sun and Earth bending space-time.

In 1915 Einstein presented a theory known as the general theory of relativity. This theory introduced a new way of understanding gravity. Einstein said that space and time are intertwined into something like a fabric. He called this fabric space-time. Space-time acts as the background for all the matter in space. This matter, including things like planets and stars, creates dents in space-time. The more massive an object is, the more it will bend space-time. When matter changes or moves, ripples are created in the space-time fabric. These ripples are gravitational waves.

Long before Einstein proposed his theory about space-time, other scientists developed theories about stars and gravity. As far back as 1783, British scientist John Michell proposed the idea that some stars could have such strong gravity that light couldn't escape. This introduced the idea of a dark star, which would eventually be known as a black hole.

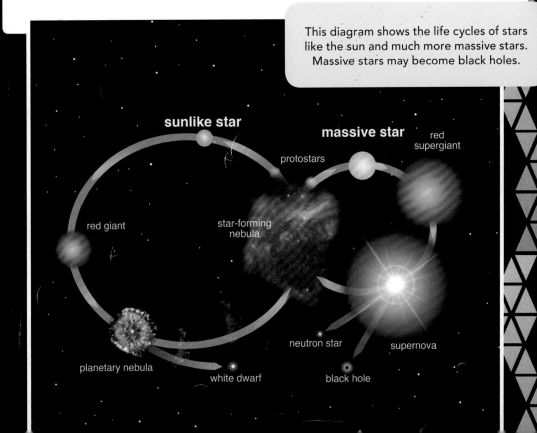

An artist's illustration shows the dark center of a black hole. John Michell first introduced the idea of a dark star in 1783.

Not all scientists agreed on the concept of a dark star. Through the centuries, there was a lot of debate about how gravity works in space and what happens to stars when they die.

This diagram shows the life cycles of stars like the sun and much more massive stars. Massive stars may become black holes.

sunlike star

massive star

red supergiant

protostars

red giant

star-forming nebula

neutron star

supernova

planetary nebula

white dwarf

black hole

Modern scientists agree that a black hole is the last stage in the life of a massive star. Throughout its life, a star has countless atoms colliding inside it. Most of the mass of an atom is in its nucleus, or center. When two or more nuclei collide, they form a new and different type of nucleus. This process is called nuclear fusion.

This image shows two hydrogen atoms fusing into one helium atom, releasing energy.

In a star, nuclear fusion usually converts hydrogen into helium. Nuclear fusion also gives off energy.

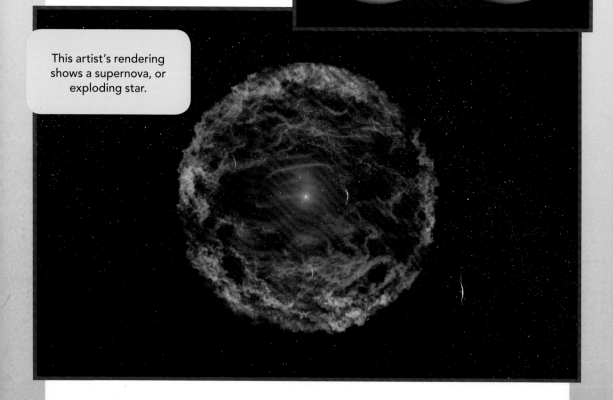

This artist's rendering shows a supernova, or exploding star.

This is what makes stars so bright and hot. After a long time, the nuclear fusion in a star stops because all the fuel has been burned up. In a massive star, all that energy has nowhere to go, so the star explodes in what is called a supernova. Parts of the outer surface of the star shoot out into space. But the star's powerful gravitational pull causes what remains to collapse in on itself. What's left is a very small object with a lot of mass—a black hole.

In 1915, around the same time Einstein introduced his ideas about space-time, a German astronomer named Karl Schwarzschild worked with Einstein's equations and proposed the idea that if enough matter were crammed into a very small area, it would produce such a strong gravitational field that light and everything else inside it would be trapped. All the mass of a black hole is compressed into an extremely dense region called the singularity. Around the

Karl Schwarzschild used Einstein's equations to further develop ideas about gravity and black holes.

singularity is a surface called the event horizon. The event horizon is also known as the point of no return because anything that passes through it toward the singularity is gone forever. Anything within the event horizon—even light—cannot escape the black hole's gravitational force.

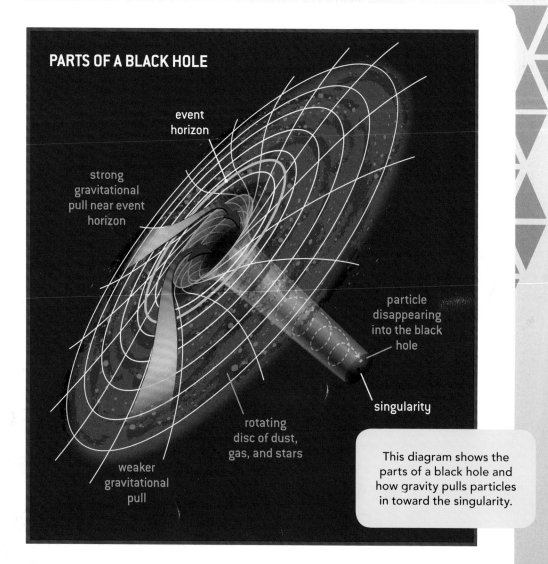

PARTS OF A BLACK HOLE

event horizon

strong gravitational pull near event horizon

particle disappearing into the black hole

singularity

rotating disc of dust, gas, and stars

weaker gravitational pull

This diagram shows the parts of a black hole and how gravity pulls particles in toward the singularity.

Throughout the twentieth century, astronomers searched for signs of black holes in outer space. Physicists tried to work out the equations to prove or disprove the theories of Einstein and other scientists. But the theories about black holes were all still ideas. No one had actually found a black hole to study and figure out if all these theories were true.

That changed in 1971. Evidence of a black hole was finally

An X-ray telescope captured this X-ray image of Cygnus X-1 in 2011. Cygnus X-1 was first discovered in 1971.

Engineers work on the first satellite launched to detect X-rays in space in 1970.

discovered when a satellite picked up X-rays coming from an invisible object. Scientists called the invisible source Cygnus X-1. Astronomers believed that the X-ray activity in Cygnus X-1 must be caused by a black hole. Though there were no images scientists could study, most astronomers agree that Cygnus X-1 was the first confirmed discovery of a black hole.

Despite this discovery, however, black holes continued to be a complex mystery within the scientific community.

Most of what scientists understood about black holes was theoretical or mathematical. Some ideas didn't quite add up. And black holes were nearly impossible to study. But as technology advanced and astronomers continued searching the skies, they began to make more discoveries about black holes, gravity, and the universe.

An optical image of the night sky shows Cygnus X-1 highlighted in a red box (*top*). This illustration of Cygnus X-1 shows how scientists believe this black hole behaves (*bottom*).

This photograph, taken by the Hubble Space Telescope, helped confirm the presence of a black hole.

Photographic Proof

In 1994 the Hubble Space Telescope focused one of its cameras on a galaxy about fifty-three million light-years from Earth. The images that the camera sent back to astronomers at the Space Telescope Science Institute in Baltimore, Maryland, confirmed something that scientists had only wondered about and debated for many years. At the center of this far-off galaxy was a disc of superhot gases swirling around an object that was incredibly massive but also very compact. That object could only be a black hole. Astronomers had discovered what they believed were black holes elsewhere in the universe prior to 1994. However, these pictures of spinning gases were the strongest evidence yet that early theories about black holes were correct.

CHAPTER 2
BLACK HOLE DETECTIVES

The LIGO site in Louisiana, with laser paths stretching away from the facility to the top and the left

The LIGO sites in Washington and Louisiana use lasers to detect gravitational waves. At each LIGO site, two lasers stretch 2.5 miles (4 kilometers) at a right angle to each other. The lasers hit a mirror and then bounce back to the center. When a gravitational wave hits the lasers, the path of one laser will be stretched slightly. The path of the other will be shortened. This change in the pattern of the lasers indicates a gravitational wave.

Scientists monitor data from the lasers in this LIGO control room.

The LIGO sites first began to search for gravitational waves in 2002. From 2010 to 2015, the sites were closed for upgrades that would make the device much more sensitive. Just three days after the facilities opened again, they detected gravitational waves.

But LIGO's work isn't finished yet. More updates are being made to help better detect gravitational waves. And a new site is being built in India to provide more data in the search to understand gravity, space-time, and black holes. Data about gravitational waves, along with information collected by various telescopes, will help give a complete picture of what goes on in and around black holes.

A LIGO technician inspects a mirror.

SEARCHING THE SKIES

Gravitational waves are one of several ways to study black holes. The other ways all involve different forms of light. But because no visible light can escape a black hole, astronomers can't study black holes through observation the way they can study stars, moons, and planets. Instead, scientists have to look for clues throughout space. Certain signs in the universe, such as a swirling disc of gases, might suggest a black hole is near. Another way to find black holes is by watching the behavior of orbiting stars. Often two stars orbit each other in what is known as a binary system. If an astronomer notices a star that seems to be orbiting around an invisible object, this is another sign that a black hole may be in the area.

But even these signs can be very difficult to detect. Often a regular telescope

This illustration shows a binary star system.

A bright white area is surrounded by a cloud of hot gas. This is a sign that a black hole might be in this area.

won't pick up on them at all. As gases move toward the black hole, they become heated to millions of degrees. The gases then give off incredibly bright X-rays. These X-rays aren't visible to the human eye or to typical telescopes, as X-ray light cannot get through Earth's atmosphere. Instead, scientists and astronomers observe black hole activity through telescopes that orbit Earth.

By being able to escape Earth's atmosphere and get a clearer look at the cosmos, these long-range telescopes can provide pictures and information that would have been impossible to imagine in Einstein's era. Orbiting telescopes can pick up X-rays, gamma rays, and visible light coming from the objects near the black hole. Astronomers can use information about the material around a black hole to learn more about its size, age, and other features such as how fast it is spinning. For example, the speed at which a star orbits a black hole gives information about how big the black hole is. By studying imagery from a variety of telescopes picking up various kinds of light waves from different locations, astronomers can put together a clear picture of black holes throughout space.

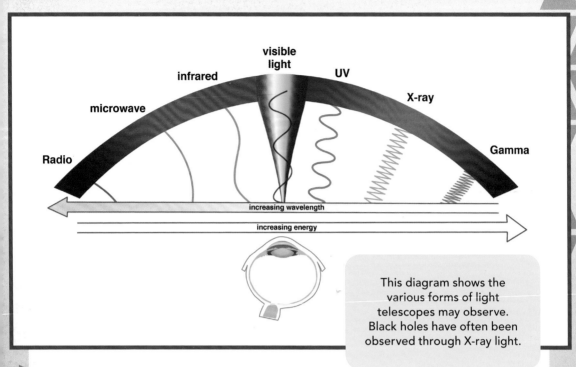

increasing wavelength

increasing energy

This diagram shows the various forms of light telescopes may observe. Black holes have often been observed through X-ray light.

HUBBLE TELESCOPE

The Hubble Space Telescope was launched in 1990. Since then it has observed countless stars, asteroids, black holes, and other phenomena in our galaxy and beyond. Because it orbits above Earth's atmosphere, it can detect much more than a telescope on Earth can. Hubble observes ultraviolet light, visible light, and near-infrared light. Hubble has been used to detect black holes. It also helps scientists study how stars and galaxies form.

Hubble has made more than one million observations. One particularly exciting observation was made in 2014.

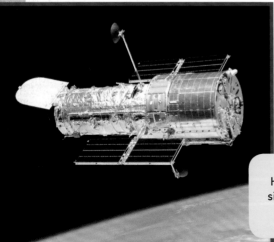

Hubble has drifted in Earth's orbit since 1990, helping scientists study stars, galaxies, and black holes.

This telescope in the South Pole is part of the Event Horizon Telescope network.

Earth-Sized Telescope

In 2015 a spacecraft sent clear, up-close pictures of Pluto to Earth. These photos revealed some surprising things about the surface of Pluto. Astronomers would like to have clear and informative pictures of black holes too.

To obtain these clear images, a telescope the size of Earth would be required. But this sort of telescope would be nearly impossible to build. Instead, astronomers are working with nine telescopes positioned around the world. Together, these telescopes will be able to imitate the effect of an Earth-sized telescope. This network of telescopes is known as the Event Horizon Telescope. All nine telescopes are expected to be online by 2018. The first three telescopes began collecting data about the supermassive black hole in the Milky Way galaxy in 2000. In 2014 one was added in Chile, and in 2015, the South Pole telescope joined the network. With each additional telescope, the imagery became clearer and scientists got closer to having an up-close picture of a black hole. Once they have a clear picture, they hope to answer questions about what happens in the area surrounding a black hole and why there are such differences in these areas among various black holes.

Hubble detected a giant black hole twenty-one million times the mass of the sun in one of the smallest but densest galaxies ever discovered. On a clear night on Earth, about four thousand stars are visible in the sky. But this galaxy is so dense with stars that if you were on a planet in that galaxy, you could look up and see a million stars in the night sky.

This illustration shows the huge black hole found by Hubble in 2014.

CHANDRA X-RAY OBSERVATORY

Chandra is a telescope that was designed to find X-rays from hot areas of space, including exploded stars and the gases around black holes. The satellite, which flies higher than the Hubble Telescope,

Chandra orbits Earth to find X-rays in space, as shown in this illustration.

An artist's depiction shows the supermassive black hole in the center of the Milky Way.

An image of the X-ray eruption from the supermassive black hole in the Milky Way, detected by Chandra

can detect X-rays from tiny particles right up until the moment they disappear into a black hole.

In the middle of the Milky Way galaxy, there is what is known as a supermassive black hole. This black hole is four million times the mass of the sun. This is actually fairly small for a supermassive black hole. This black hole is not usually very active. But in 2013 and 2014, Chandra detected the largest eruptions of X-rays ever recorded from the black hole. Astronomers suggested that the X-rays may have been caused by an asteroid that flew too close to the black hole and was ripped to shreds. It's still not clear what caused the big burst of energy from the black hole, but Chandra is still watching, and it is always looking for more exciting events.

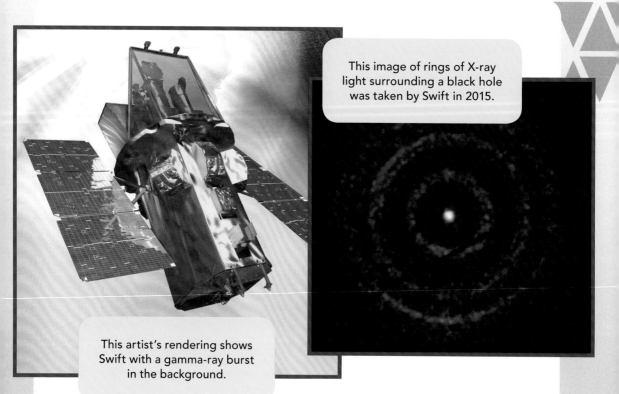

This image of rings of X-ray light surrounding a black hole was taken by Swift in 2015.

This artist's rendering shows Swift with a gamma-ray burst in the background.

SWIFT

The Swift Gamma-Ray Burst Mission was launched in 2004. The Swift orbiting observatory was designed to learn more about the bursts of gamma radiation that can be observed throughout the universe. Swift uses three telescopes to observe gamma-ray bursts (GRBs) and their afterglow through gamma ray, X-ray, ultraviolet, and visible light. Scientists wonder if GRBs are signs of a new black hole forming or if they are caused by some other powerful and violent event. In July 2015, Swift captured images of circles of X-ray light surrounding a black hole. These images will tell astronomers more about the matter around black holes.

Along with these orbiting telescopes, Earthbound observatories are also crucial to the study of black holes and other objects in space.

An observatory on the Canary Islands is home to the world's largest telescope (*top*). This telescope in Hawaii is one of two telescopes that make up the Gemini Observatory, which allows astronomers to observe the entire night sky (*left*).

Astronomers in observatories around the world often work together and share information. By sharing data and information, astronomers can come up with more complete images and theories about the events occurring in space. There are giant telescopes in Arizona, in Hawaii, on Spain's Canary Islands off the coast of northwestern Africa, in Puerto Rico, and in South Africa.

CHAPTER 3
BREAKING BLACK HOLE NEWS

This artist's depiction shows the supermassive black hole discovered in a small galaxy in 2016.

Often when scientists do their work, they are trying to prove theories or find real-world applications for their ideas and calculations. But sometimes as scientists study data and examine imagery from telescopes, they make discoveries that disprove their theories or take the scientists completely by surprise.

SMALL-TOWN SKYSCRAPER

In 2016 astronomers found a black hole that is two hundred million light-years away from Earth. The black hole is seventeen billion times the mass of the sun. But what really surprised scientists about this black hole is that it was found in a small galaxy. Some scientists say that the discovery is like seeing a skyscraper in a small town—instead of in a large city, where it would be expected.

The black hole discovered in 2016 is seventeen billion times the mass of the sun (*above*).

This image of a supermassive black hole was created by information from Hubble and a radio telescope.

These two galaxies are in the process of merging. Scientists originally thought this was the only way giant black holes formed.

This spiral galaxy contains a supermassive black hole.

Originally, scientists thought that the largest black holes formed and became larger when galaxies and other black holes collided. These collisions allow the black hole to take in a lot of gas and dust and merge with other black holes. But with the discovery of this new supermassive black hole, scientists are beginning to think that there may be more than one way black holes are made.

"What this is saying is that you don't need these galaxy clusters to grow very massive black holes," said Poshak Gandhi, an astronomer and professor at the University of Southampton in England. "That throws a wrench in the works of our understanding of how these monster black holes form—it throws the field wide open."

The discovery also means that more black holes may be in the universe than astronomers previously thought. Originally, scientists thought there might be a black hole at the center of every large galaxy, but now it appears that supermassive black holes can exist in smaller galaxies too. Researchers are working to find out what else besides the size of a galaxy might determine the mass of a black hole.

Some scientists also wonder if this black hole is actually two black holes that are circling each other and

A galaxy thought to contain two supermassive black holes is shown in this Hubble image (*top*). An artist's rendering shows what two circling black holes might look like (*bottom*).

that will eventually collide and merge. If this is the case, it may be producing gravitational waves that researchers such as those at LIGO would be excited to study.

▶ POWER OF A THOUSAND SUNS

Although black holes are often understood as objects that suck in everything near them and never let anything out, black holes are often seen shooting off blasts of gases and debris in what are called particle jets. These jets are incredibly bright, and they move almost as fast as the speed of light.

accretion disk

toward earth

particle jet

innermost stable
circular orbit (ISCO)

source of quasi-periodic
oscillation (QPO)

This image shows a supermassive black hole with a particle jet.

A black hole consumes a nearby star in this illustration (*top*). Scientists observed this red flash of light coming from a black hole (*right*).

In June 2015, astronomers observed strong, red flashes of light coming from a black hole as it consumed the star orbiting it. Scientists studying the event said that each flash was quick but "blindingly intense, equivalent to the power output of about 1,000 suns."

The scientists determined that the flashes were produced when the black hole could not consume all the matter available from the orbiting star. Instead, it flung the extra matter away from itself.

This is not the first time an event such as this has happened. But these black hole outbursts are rare and unpredictable. The last time this particular black hole shot off like this was in 1989. Scientists are excited to study similar outbursts. They believe it will help them understand more about how black holes and their particle jets are formed. The continued study will require scientists around the world to work together to capture data and make observations.

Scientists have discovered a few other things about particle jets. In 2016 scientists observed a particle jet that reached an incredible 18 trillion°F (10 trillion°C). They had thought that the hottest these jets would be able to get was 179 billion°F (99 billion°C). The scientists have said they will need to do more research to understand particle jets and what makes them so hot.

Around the same time as the superhot jets were found, scientists in South Africa noticed some strange behavior in several black holes that spanned a large area in space. The jets of these black holes all pointed in the same direction. The astronomers who made this observation were very surprised. Nothing in their research or theories predicted something like this. "This is not obviously expected based on our current understanding of cosmology. It's a bizarre finding," said Romeel Davé, a professor at the University of the Western Cape in South Africa. Astronomers say that the only

This illustration shows a particle jet shooting out from a black hole.

Scientists continue to study how particle jets are formed and how they are affected by the spin of the black hole.

way for this alignment to occur is if all of these black holes are spinning in the same direction. As astronomers continue to study these black holes, they hope to discover more about how and when the black holes—and even the universe—formed.

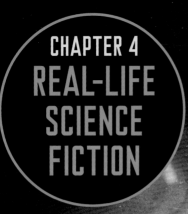

CHAPTER 4
REAL-LIFE SCIENCE FICTION

Scientists believe that the supermassive black hole at the center of this galaxy produces powerful particle jets.

In many ways, black holes might seem like something from a movie. The ideas of ripples in space-time, swirling gases that give off X-rays, and invisible objects that shoot out incredibly hot particle jets across space seem unreal. Yet many of the theories about black holes and the universe have been proven to be true. And there are other seemingly crazy theories about black holes that could be true too.

STEPHEN HAWKING'S HAIR

One of the most famous physicists in the world is Stephen Hawking. Much of his work has been related to black holes. In the 1970s, Hawking theorized that black holes may become small over time and could eventually even disappear. He said that black holes emit radiation. This radiation became known as Hawking radiation. Because black holes give off this radiation, they lose mass and can eventually evaporate altogether. However, this idea was problematic for scientists. According to the laws of physics, information can never entirely disappear. But in Hawking's theory, when black holes consume matter, they also consume all the information about that matter. When the black holes disappear, then all that information would be completely lost.

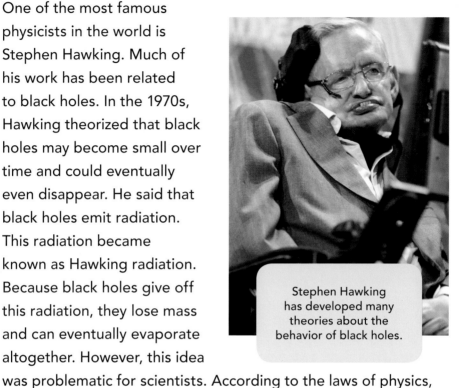

Stephen Hawking has developed many theories about the behavior of black holes.

This artist's rendering shows a space probe approaching a black hole to study Hawking radiation.

In 2015 Hawking developed a new theory to help solve this problem. He said that instead of information being stored inside black holes and eventually disappearing, maybe the information is stored on the outside of a black hole. The idea is that on the event horizon, wrinkles in space-time—or "hairs," as Hawking called them—store the information about everything that has passed through it. Then the information would be able to escape the black hole as Hawking radiation—but the information would still be scrambled and useless.

Other scientists say that Hawking's new theory doesn't necessarily solve the problem of lost information. But it does give them some new ideas to work with.

INFORMATION LEAK

Another theory developed in 2016 by a scientist named Chris Adami offers a different solution. Adami's research says that black holes do not destroy information. Instead, information is able to

Chris Adami (*pointing*) discusses equations with a student. Adami and other scientists use computer models to help them understand complex ideas such as information leak (*right*).

leak out of a black hole over time. Through mathematical tools and computers, Adami simulated the life of a black hole. In the simulations, information was found outside of the black holes.

These calculations also helped prove another old theory about black holes. This theory said that black holes have curves. These curves would allow information to enter and then exit a black hole. Adami's calculations were the first to show something similar.

WHAT ABOUT WORMHOLES?

Hawking also came up with another theory about where information goes after entering a black hole. This theory says that maybe the information escapes—into an alternate universe.

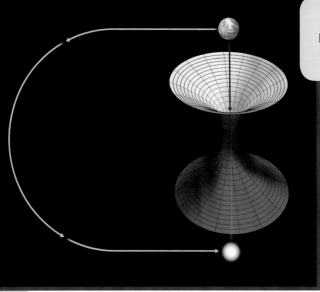

Scientists agree that wormholes, like the one depicted here between Earth and a star, are possible.

Hawking said that some ideas about black holes suggest that such a universe could be possible. But the information would never be able to come back into its original universe.

This idea gets at a question that has been common about black holes and that often shows up in science fiction: What would happen if you fell into a black hole? Generally, scientists have agreed that matter that enters a black hole would be stretched like spaghetti until it rips apart. This matter then joins the black hole's event horizon and eventually leaves as Hawking radiation. But entrance into an alternate world through a wormhole is not impossible. Einstein's theories even allow for it.

Black holes bend space intensely toward the singularity in a deep, steep, never-ending curve. If a black hole is also spinning, this means that the singularity could be a ring. This ring could in turn be a wormhole through space and time. This wormhole is what might allow information to escape into another universe. Wormholes also open up ideas about time travel. It's a fascinating concept that has captured the imaginations of many. But scientists have a hard time working out the mathematics to say how such a thing would really work or be stable. Many agree that wormholes are possible. But they are also highly unlikely.

WHAT'S NEXT?

Research and knowledge about black holes change every day as scientists develop new theories, make new discoveries, and release new technology. Each new idea helps scientists learn more about black holes—how they are formed, what's inside of them, and what might happen to them over time. Scientists also continue to learn about the universe itself and how galaxies, stars, and planetary systems formed and change. The earliest theories and ideas about the universe and the laws of gravity and physics continue to be challenged, developed, or proven.

When LIGO made its discovery of gravitational waves in 2015, a whole new way of looking at the universe opened up that will make way for even more discoveries and knowledge.

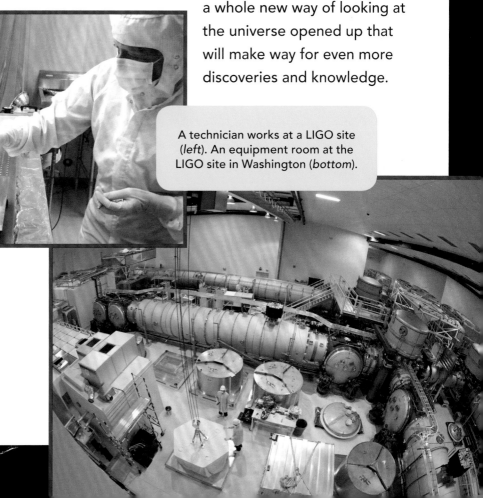

A technician works at a LIGO site (*left*). An equipment room at the LIGO site in Washington (*bottom*).

According to Gabriela González, a professor at Louisiana State University (which was closely involved in LIGO's research), "The detection [of gravitational waves] is the beginning of a new era. The field of gravitational wave astronomy is now a reality."

In the months following the first detection of gravitational waves, those working on LIGO planned to make the detector even more sensitive. LIGO scientists predicted that LIGO would be able to detect between ten and one hundred more black hole collisions. Some scientists have even begun searching for places in the universe where two black holes may be orbiting each other. They are working on predicting where and when these black holes might merge, creating gravitational waves.

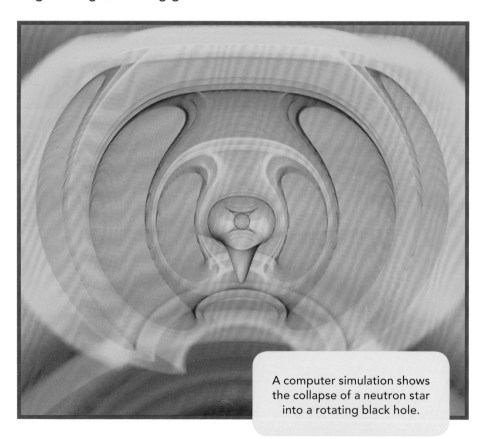

A computer simulation shows the collapse of a neutron star into a rotating black hole.

Luciano Rezzolla (*top*) is one of the researchers who came up with the formula to determine the maximum mass of a neutron star. This image depicts the remains of a collapsed star (*right*).

Other scientists are working on predicting when stars might collapse, forming black holes. A group of scientists in Germany have come up with calculations to determine the maximum mass a neutron star can have before it collapses into a black hole. This information will help scientists find black holes to study throughout the universe so that they can learn and understand the amazing universe and the real-life science fiction of black holes.

Source Notes

7   Calla Cofield, "Gravitational Waves: What Their Discovery Means for Science and Humanity," *Space.com*, February 12, 2016, http://www.space.com/31922-gravitational-waves-detection-what-it-means.html.

8   Ibid.

31   Jason Daley, "Supermassive Black Holes May Be More Common Than Previously Thought," *Smithsonian.com*, April 7, 2016, http://www.smithsonianmag.com/smart-news/supermassive-black-holes-may-be-more-common-previously-thought-180958688/#1V9K0SZu4e9gmvqw.99.

33   Josh Hrala, "Astronomers Have Observed a Black Hole Flashing Red with the Energy of 1,000 Suns," *Science Alert*, March 18, 2016, http://www.sciencealert.com/astronomers-have-witnessed-a-black-hole-flash-red-with-the-energy-of-1-000-suns.

34   Ian O'Neill, "'Bizarre' Group of Distant Black Holes Are Mysteriously Aligned," *Discovery News*, April 12, 2016, http://news.discovery.com/space/astronomy/bizarre-group-of-distant-black-holes-are-mysteriously-aligned-160412.htm.

42   "LIGO Facility Livingston Confirms Gravitational Waves Detected 100 Years after Einstein Predicted Them," *BusinessReport*, February 11, 2016, https://www.businessreport.com/article/ligo-facility-livingston-confirms-gravitational-waves-detected-100-years-einstein-predicted.

LERNER

Expand learning beyond the printed book. Download free, complementary educational resources for this book from our website, www.lerneresource.com.

SOURCE

Glossary

black hole: an invisible area in outer space with gravity so strong that light cannot get out of it

event horizon: the imaginary boundary around a black hole beyond which nothing can escape

gravitational wave: a ripple in space-time that happens when two massive objects, such as black holes, merge together

light-year: a unit of distance equal to the distance that light travels in one year

matter: the stuff that forms physical objects and occupies space

merge: to become joined or united

Milky Way: the galaxy that includes our solar system

nucleus: the central part of an atom. *Nuclei* is the plural of *nucleus.*

orbit: to travel around something such as a planet or moon in a curved path

satellite: a natural or human-made object that orbits another object in space

singularity: the compressed point in a black hole with a huge mass and powerful gravitational pull

space-time: the concept of space and time combined into one entity

theory: an idea or set of ideas that is meant to explain facts or events

Selected Bibliography

Castelvecchi, Davide. "The Black Hole Collision That Reshaped Physics." *Scientific American*, March 24, 2016. http://www.scientificamerican.com /article/the-black-hole-collision-that-reshaped-physics.

Fromme, Alison. "Our Man at LIGO." *Mountain Home*, February 26, 2016. http://mountainhomemag.com/people-life/our-man-at-ligo/.

Lewin, Sarah. "Supermassive Black Hole Found in Unlikely Cosmic Backwater." *Scientific American*, April 7, 2016. http://www.scientificamerican.com /article/supermassive-black-hole-found-in-unlikely-cosmic-backwater.

Mann, Adam. "A Brief History of Mind-Bending Ideas about Black Holes." *Wired*, January 29, 2014. http://www.wired.com/2014/01/brief-history-of -black-holes.

"Black Holes." NASA. Accessed June 6, 2016. http://science.nasa.gov /astrophysics/focus-areas/black-holes.

Further Reading

Aguilar, David A. *Space Encyclopedia: A Tour of Our Solar System and Beyond*. Washington, DC: National Geographic, 2013.

Black Holes: Gravity's Relentless Pull
http://hubblesite.org/explore_astronomy/black_holes/home.html

Carson, Mary Kay. *Beyond the Solar System: Exploring Galaxies, Black Holes, Alien Planets, and More*. Chicago: Chicago Review Press, 2013.

DeCristofano, Carolyn Cinami. *A Black Hole Is Not a Hole*. Watertown, MA: Charlesbridge, 2012.

NASA: What Is a Black Hole?
http://www.nasa.gov/audience/forstudents/5-8/features/nasa-knows/what -is-a-black-hole-58.html

Roland, James. *Pluto: A Space Discovery Guide*. Minneapolis: Lerner Publications, 2017.

Index

Photo Acknowledgments

The images in this book are used with the permission of: NASA, S. Gezari (Johns Hopkins University), and J. Guillochon (University of California, Santa Cruz), p. 2; Caltech/MIT/LIGO Lab, pp. 4, 5 (both), 18, 19 (top), 41 (both); Axel Mellinger/Caltech/MIT/LIGO Lab, p. 6; © Bridgeman Images, p. 7 (top); R. Hurt/Caltech-JPL/NASA, p. 7 (bottom); © PASIEKA/Getty Images, p. 8; ESO/M. Kornmesser, p. 9 (top); ESO/L. Calçada/M.Kornmesser, p. 9 (bottom); T. Pyle/Caltech/MIT/LIGO Lab, p. 10; © iStockphoto.com/gmutlu, p. 11 (top); NASA and the Night Sky Network, p. 11 (bottom); © Heywoody/Dreamstime.com, p. 12 (top); NASA, ESA, and G. Bacon (STScI), pp. 12 (bottom), 20 (top), 31 (bottom); © AIP Emilio Segre Visual Archives, courtesy Martin Schwarzschild, p. 13; © Laura Westlund/Independent Picture Service, p. 14; NASA/CXC, pp. 15 (both), 22 (bottom), 24 (bottom), 38; NASA/CXC/M. Weiss, pp. 16 (both), 25 (top); © NASA/ESA/STSCI/H. Ford et al/Science Source, p. 17; Heintze/Caltech/MIT/LIGO Lab, p. 19 (bottom); NASA/CXC/KIPAC/S. Allen et al. Radio: NRAO/VLA/G. Taylor, Infrared: NASA/ESA/McMaster Univ/W. Harris, p. 20 (bottom); ESA/NASA & R. Sahai, p. 21 (top); JAXA, p. 21 (bottom); © Spencer Sutton/Science Source, p. 22 (top); John Mallon III/National Science Foundation, p. 23; NASA, ESA, STScI-PRC14-41a, p. 24 (top); NASA/CXC/Stanford/I. Zhuravleva et al., p. 25 (bottom); Spectrum and NASA E/PO, Sonoma State University, Aurore Simonnet, p. 26 (left); Andrew Beardmore (Univ of Leicester) and NASA/Swift, p. 26 (right); © iStockphoto.com/AlexanderNikiforov, p. 27 (top); © iStockphoto.com/EduardMoldoveanuPhotography, p. 27 (bottom); NASA, ESA, D. Coe, J. Anderson, and R. van der Marel (STScI), p. 28; NASA/SDO, p. 29 (top); NASA, ESA, S. Baum & C. O'Dea (RIT), R. Perley & W. Cotton (NRAO/AUI/NSF), and the Hubble Heritage Team (STScI/AURA), p. 29 (bottom); ESO, p. 30 (top); ESA/Hubble & NASA, p. 30 (bottom); NASA, ESA, the Hubble Heritage Team (STScI/AURA)-ESA/Hubble Collaboration, and A. Evans (University of Virginia, Charlottesville/NRAO/Stony Brook University), p. 31 (top); NASA/Goddard Space Flight Center, p. 32; ESO/L. Calçada, pp. 33 (top), 34; DSS2/sky-map.org/Poshak Gandhi et al, p. 33 (bottom); NASA/JPL-Caltech, p. 35; X-ray: NASA/CXC/Caltech/P Ogle et al. Optical: NASA/STScI. IR: NASA/JPL-Caltech. Radio: NSF/NRAO/VLA, p. 36; Dennis Van Tine/Abacapress.com/Newscom, p. 37 (top); © Richard Kail/Science Source, p. 37 (bottom); © Michigan State University, p. 39 (both); © Gary Hincks/Science Source, p. 40; © Prof. Dr. Luciano Rezzolla, pp. 42, 43 (left); NASA/CXC/SAO/T. Temim et al, IR: NASA/JPL-Caltech, p. 43 (right).

Cover: © Mark Garlick/Science Photo Library/Getty Images.